BITCOIN AND CRYPTOCURRENCY TRADING FOR BEGINNERS 2021:

Basic information, encrypted exchanges, graphics and trading advice

ISBN: 9798731271301

CONTENTS

Introduction

What is Blockchain?

Blockchain is a decentralised database technology that allows people to register a digital record or transaction for something they want to keep private or secure.

As such, blockchain can be used to store and process digital data securely, with anyone having access to the ledger and verification system that tracks that data.

When a person uses blockchain technology to handle and store their information, they don't need to rely on a third-party, such as Facebook, to protect their data.

It allows users to have complete control over who can see and access certain information, and are also able to achieve greater transparency into the organisation that they are operating within.

Who is using blockchain?

Bitcoin gained popularity for being a currency used to transfer value around the world that does not have the same restrictions as a traditional currency (such as being controlled by a central bank).

As well as being a form of payment, Bitcoin is also a digital currency that is only linked to a particular bitcoin address.

For example, a consumer with one bitcoin could buy goods from another consumer with bitcoin, or a bitcoin address could be used to buy bitcoin from another address.

Once a specific bitcoin address is established for a particular transaction, the seller is able to send the bitcoin to that address, which will only accept that particular transaction, resulting in the transaction to become public once complete.

Bitcoin uses a secure peer-to-peer network called blockchain which means that a person cannot see another person's bitcoin balance.

Many organisations, such as IBM, are exploring the use of blockchain in different applications.

What are the best cryptocurrency exchanges?

Looking to acquire cryptocurrency? The best cryptocurrency exchanges for buying and selling Bitcoin and other crypto coins are listed below.

Most of these exchanges are direct (or offer direct acceptance to all cryptocurrencies) or semi-direct (they accept some cryptocurrencies but not others).

In order to buy and sell cryptocurrencies, you need a digital wallet, which is basically a saving account to hold your cryptocurrency. Depending on how many you have, it can be all you need.

If you want to buy coins directly from the exchange, you'll have to pay transaction fees, which may vary according to the exchange. For example, Coinbase charges a 3% fee to sell coins on its platform.

At the moment the leading and most well-known cryptocurrency exchange is Coinbase. It provides a seamless, safe and secure platform to buy and sell cryptocurrencies.

It was founded by Fred Ehrsam and Brian Armstrong in June 2012, and it offers a wide variety of services, ranging from Bitcoin and Litecoin to Ethereum and many more.

Coinbase was one of the first platforms to accept Bitcoin, and it currently also accepts Bitcoin Cash and Litecoin. In 2017 it also made Bitcoin trades available to Australian customers.

Coinbase app

Head on over to Coinbase to buy Bitcoin, Litecoin, Ethereum or any other cryptocurrencies. Before you can do so, you need a Coinbase account.

When you create your account, Coinbase asks you to enter a US bank account or a credit or debit card for the account to work. However, it's also possible to purchase Bitcoin using PayPal, Google Wallet, Mastercard or Visa.

It's also important to note that Coinbase accounts are not insured by any kind of guarantee. Coinbase also accepts deposits in foreign bank accounts, but you'll have to provide the relevant ID to do so.

If you wish to withdraw the purchased coins, you can do so in a number of ways. You can do so through wire transfer or SEPA (the European Union's electronic real-time gross settlement system).

The latter allows you to purchase a variety of currencies, including Bitcoin. You'll also need a linked bank account and a SEPA-enabled payment method in order to withdraw your cryptocurrency.

Coinbase payment methods

In addition to acquiring cryptocurrencies, Coinbase also offers a wide variety of payment methods. You can pay with debit cards, credit cards and bank accounts.

You can also send money from your Coinbase wallet to other accounts or wallets. In 2017 it also allowed you to send Bitcoin using the PayPal account you created at the time of your account registration.

A Coinbase wallet is the name given to an account used to store digital coins. It is basically a private or public key, a unique string of numbers, that you use to own Bitcoin or other crypto assets.

There is also a trade desk (Coinbase Trade) in which you can store your purchased digital assets. It is basically a type of trading platform where you can sell and buy crypto.

Coinbase trade desk

As of today, there are over 70 million coins available on Coinbase Trade. This means that almost everybody with a wallet or a verified email address can trade cryptocurrencies.

Coinbase trade desk offers the best trading experience for the average trader, and it offers low fees in comparison to other exchanges.

Of course, the main advantage of a Coinbase Trade desk is that you can use your wallet to trade all the crypto assets you own, rather than having to buy and sell new coins every time.

Even though Coinbase is now accepting Bitcoin Cash and Litecoin, you can also use the platform to purchase and sell Bitcoin. Additionally, you can use it to make payments and to send and receive Bitcoin Cash, Litecoin and Ethereum.

Coinbase payment methods and conversion rates

Coinbase allows you to convert various cryptocurrencies to USD and EUR using its built-in exchange. It allows you to use all major fiat currencies (EUR, USD, GBP, AUD, CAD, SEK, EUR, NOK, CHF, HKD, NZD, SGD and ZAR).

Cryptocurrency to fiat exchange rates are readily available in the Coinbase dashboard. If you want to purchase a crypto asset in USD or EUR and convert it to fiat, it's as simple as selecting the option of conversion and setting the desired rate.

Coinbase also provides conversion rates in the currencies available on the platform. This means that you can convert

Bitcoin, Litecoin, Ethereum or any other available crypto assets to your chosen fiat currency.

The transaction costs depend on the payment methods you use, the country you are in, the transaction amount, the frequency of buying and selling, the amount of money in your Coinbase wallet and the speed of your internet connection.

Fiat to crypto currency conversion rates are in the order of 25% to 75%, depending on the payment method you select and the country of purchase. In some countries such as Switzerland and the US, this can be significantly higher.

Exchanging cryptocurrencies to fiat

Coinbase exchange rates have a maximum 'conversion premium' in certain countries. It varies between 10% and 30% depending on the country and the rate of exchange.

It's important to note that the premium depends not only on the conversion rate and the currency in which you wish to convert, but also on the status of your Bitcoin and Ethereum wallet.

Basically, as long as you are using a valid Coinbase wallet to buy and sell digital assets, the conversion premium should be below 10%, but in some countries it can be quite high, such as Switzerland, the US, the UK, Denmark and Singapore.

Considering that a popular strategy is to exchange cryptocurrencies to fiat, as soon as the price of a cryptocurrency or a currency appreciates to a significant level, you will have the opportunity to take advantage of the conversion premium to profit from the subsequent appreciation.

Cryptocurrencies and finance: keys to the future?

As we are talking about Bitcoin and other cryptocurrencies, we must also look at the huge potential that they have to affect the current financial system and the global economy in general.

When it comes to ICOs, we have yet to see the true potential of a cryptocurrency company that doesn't have much cash to spend on advertising. It's obvious that some cryptocurrencies can raise funds in a much quicker way.

According to some estimates, the global cryptocurrency market, including Bitcoin, Ethereum and other coins, is currently worth $200 billion. If only one in ten companies chooses to launch an ICO, they might raise the full amount of funding needed.

This brings to mind the question of who really has the

potential to create a successful ICO. It can be individuals or funds with a broad financial network and a huge amount of experience.

Could you imagine if a fund organized a successful ICO and received investments worth $20 billion?

Alternatively, it's very possible that decentralized companies will generate a large amount of money and win the competition of fundraising.

According to some experts, it's very possible that the financial market could grow by a factor of 10 in the next 10 years. This could lead to the creation of many exciting investment opportunities that blockchain technologies are not capable of offering today.

Overall, it looks like the money raised by ICOs is not something that ICO investors should lose their interest in. According to some studies, this year more than 1,500 ICOs will launch.

Considering that investments in new tokens or startups raised via ICOs grew by over 100% last year, and that they raised $1.8 billion in 2017, a successful token offering has great chances to make a considerable impact on the market, and its share of market value will be larger than it is today.

The digital revolution and the ICO phenomenon

As cryptocurrency and ICOs continue to become more and more mainstream, the developments of the digital revolution are now becoming clearer. In an interview with me in the Swissinfo earlier this year, Charles Hoskinson, an expert on Ethereum, confirmed my thesis:

"Some of the basic ideas behind ICOs are the development of the Internet, which was funded by ICOs and was successfully developed. The creation of startups through ICOs has proved itself many times over and now that they have proven themselves, we're going to see even more companies go to ICOs to raise funding and to create their companies. It's a very similar market to what we saw with crowdfunding."

Similarly, Ruben Pacheco, an analyst for digital currencies at Digital Asset Research, told me in an interview that he expects that at least 10% of all initial coin offerings in the market will be conducted through a sale of tokens. This means that the tokens issued through ICOs could easily account for more than $5 billion in market capitalization.

Moreover, a survey conducted by CoinSchedule suggested that if one looks at the market potential of ICOs, one could easily conclude that one could raise more than $30 billion if all ICOs were held through an auction.

Overall, we've seen many people investing in ICOs this year, and probably they will continue to do so. It is not yet clear whether it will generate the financial and investment capital that the market needs or whether the companies that will launch ICOs will be the ones that will truly thrive. But, for now, the ICO trend seems to have great potential.

It's very likely that it will continue to evolve and will ultimately bring about many changes in the digital financial world.

Chapter 1 How did Blockchain connect with cryptocurrencies?

Blockchain is the underlying technology that cryptocurrencies are built on. It's a digital, distributed database that has no central authority, which can be used to record the transactions that create a cryptocurrency.

The Blockchain of a cryptocurrency is a decentralized ledger that every person on the network can see at all times. The benefit to using Blockchain is that there is no central authority, which means there is no fraud. That eliminates the chance of hacking and the loss of funds.

The true value of Blockchain to a business, however, is how it simplifies and speeds up their processes and transactions. Blockchain brings transparency to business transactions because the public can see every transaction as it's happening.

It also brings efficiency, as transactions can be made more quickly. The result is lower transaction costs for a business.

What are some of the opportunities and threats of Blockchain?

Blockchain is a global technology that's disruptive to many

industries because it's a decentralized form of data. That means that it's not owned by a company. Instead, every user can take part in the transactions.

The fundamental disruptor is that a company that isn't used to everyone having access to the same data is in for a rude awakening. This is a bit of a head scratcher for some companies, but it can be an opportunity for new companies to jump in and grab some of the market share.

It's also a source of threat because criminals can easily create fraudulent transactions to try and steal money or other valuables. There have already been several thefts of cryptocurrency like in the case of Coinye or the CoinyeCoin.

How does Bitcoin fit into Blockchain?

Bitcoin is a cryptocurrency that is mostly associated with Blockchain. It's a digital currency and it's what's referred to as a "cryptocurrency."

In Bitcoin, "crypto" means encrypted data. Cryptocurrency is a type of decentralized currency in which all transactions are carried out using cryptographic methods. The currency is also decentralized, meaning that there is no central authority that issues the currency. Instead, it's created through the hard work of computer miners.

What are some of the risks with Bitcoin?

Bitcoin has become so popular that there are now many ways to obtain it. It's becoming a major choice in cyberattacks because the number of digital wallets is growing. This has happened through the various schemes of Bitcoin hackers. They use a "mempool" to automatically scoop up transactions and immediately claim the coin without anyone's approval.

Hackers can also steal customers' Bitcoins if they gain access to a customer's email address. They'll use the customer's email address to set up an account for a Bitcoin purchase.

Another major risk is the fact that there is no central authority that regulates Bitcoin transactions or creates new Bitcoins. This results in Bitcoin being under the control of individual miners. Miners can mine a coin, but they can also create fake transactions and take some of the coin.

How do you use Blockchain?

Blockchain is a central technology for cryptocurrencies and a whole host of other technologies. It's the underlying technology that bitcoin and other cryptocurrency is built on.

Blockchain works in a similar way to cloud technology in that you can store different kinds of information in a database. Each time someone creates a transaction with a new transaction, the database will generate a new block of data and connect it to the previous block. This creates a chain of blocks and each new block is added to the last.

Each block must have a fixed number of transactions in them. The number of transactions needed is known to a user who could create transactions in each block. This is known as "proof of work."

This is the fundamental method of carrying out a Bitcoin transaction. It's what's known as mining because there are always miners working to create blocks of transactions.

Every block contains a key that only a computer can use. The computer must solve a complex equation and the key will unlock the transaction, adding that transaction to the chain. The block with the block key can be added to the chain, which is called the "block chain."

It's also important to know that, according to BlockVerify, "proof of work" can be defeated by the use of "proof of stake." In this type of system, the computers that are working to confirm the transactions are not directly running the calculations but they're helping to protect other computers that are running the mining algorithm.

What are other uses of Blockchain?

Blockchain can be used in a wide variety of ways. One example is in identity management. This can be done in both public and private records. In public records, people can know which places a person has visited through the blockchain. The blockchain is used to keep track of when a person was there.

Blockchain can also be used to verify online retailers. The retailer's platform is updated using a special form of encryption so that anyone who is on the blockchain network can know which products are sold.

Companies use blockchain in the security field to show how goods have been delivered. They can also track all of the parts used in a product to ensure it has not been tampered with.

There's also a lot of interest in blockchain in the medical field. Companies are using the blockchain to store medical records and keep track of prescriptions. Blockchain also could be used to keep track of the authenticity of the drugs a person is taking.

Some companies have started using blockchain to store contracts and to maintain the integrity of the underlying technology. This has led to projects such as a trustless alternative to Amazon, called "Fang," that will let companies store digital documents on the Ethereum network.

How are companies using blockchain?

Blockchain is especially popular with companies that are trying to comply with regulations. For example, a car manufacturer is using blockchain to show where every part in the car has been made.

Estonia is using blockchain to keep track of benefits and pensions of its citizens. Australia has used it to track the sale of its electricity. And the Commonwealth Bank of Australia is using the technology to prove that any trade credit fraud is legitimate.

With the security blockchain offers, it's becoming a popular way for retailers to keep their customers' data safe. As it grows, it's likely that you'll start to see more companies using it to store this data, too.

What are some other uses of Blockchain?

While you may know blockchain as the technology behind Bitcoin, it's actually much more than that. It's used for a whole range of purposes. Here are some of the more popular uses.

Supply Chain Management

Supply chain management is also known as logistics management. It's about getting products from a manufacturer to a retailer to your home. Blockchain makes it possible to get more of that process done in a way that's easier for both the manufacturer and the retailer.

One example is using blockchain for tracking the shipments from a manufacturer to a retailer. Each block on the blockchain is associated with a specific place a product was created. This makes it easier for companies to keep track of the amount of time it takes a product to make it to a store and, more importantly, the products' travels to make it there.

Privacy

Another common use of blockchain is protecting the privacy of people's personal information. This isn't always the case, though. If you use any online service, chances are it will use some form of encryption to protect that data. Even Apple uses blockchain to encrypt private messages.

Takeaways

If you're interested in how blockchain works, you can learn more about it at Stanford University's website. You can also find a more detailed explanation of how the technology works at MIT's website. If you want to learn about all of the applications of blockchain, Stanford University's website has a guide to nearly 100 possible applications of the technology.

There are a lot of different ways blockchain is being used. Here are a few ways you can keep an eye on it to see what else it can be used for.

The federal government is considering using blockchain technology to make a single government database for all of its files. A company called ConsenSys has already developed a system that's used to store and store records with the intention of simplifying the process of transferring those records. Because the ledger is stored on the public Ethereum network, that makes it harder for a hacker to make off with the records. Other companies are also using blockchain in a big way for things such as making online betting more transparent.

What are some other ways blockchain is changing the world?

Blockchain technology could change the way the government operates and how you use online services. Here are a few ways you can keep an eye on the evolution of blockchain.

How will blockchain change education?

Blockchain technology could eventually be used to make sure students' educational records are kept more securely than ever before. For instance, the country of Estonia uses blockchain to make sure student records are updated as they progress through school. The system also allows students to make real-time payments to their teachers.

In the U.S., large colleges are using blockchain technology to help students learn, as well. The University of California is implementing a blockchain platform for online course management, among other uses. More than 15 universities are also using blockchain-based college grading systems, but there's a big downside. Some of the systems out there are essentially centralized databases. That means they can be hacked and put students' grades at risk. You can read more about the current state of blockchain in education at MIT.

How will blockchain change health care?

Even the technology used to run online medical records could be using blockchain. This includes EHRs, which is short for electronic health records. These systems allow doctors and other health professionals to keep all of their records together. Patients and insurance companies can also see all of the records, which can be helpful in making health decisions. If more doctors and companies used blockchain to help with healthcare records, it could go a long way to helping patients with difficult medical problems.

Now that you know more about how blockchain is being used in many industries, it's time to look at some ways it could affect your personal life.

Chapter 2 Cryptocurrencies

What are cryptocurrencies?

Cryptocurrencies such as bitcoin are decentralized digital assets that work on a digital ledger or database known as the blockchain.

In the blockchain, every transaction is recorded and time stamped, making it virtually impossible to go back and alter transactions, or to counterfeit them.

The decentralized nature of cryptocurrencies also makes them resilient to online theft because there is no central authority that could halt the entire network, or seize assets as has been done in the case of cryptocurrencies bitcoin and litecoin.

Why are cryptocurrencies valuable?

Because they offer an asset-backed currency in a rapidly digitizing world, cryptocurrency markets have attracted a huge investor base.

In contrast to the traditional fiat currencies issued by the national government, cryptocurrencies are not legal tender and are not backed by any government authority. They are not issued by any entity.

That said, cryptocurrency prices have surged in the past few months, with bitcoin, the most well-known digital currency, trading at $5,580 on Friday afternoon.

While bitcoin has gained mainstream recognition, it has attracted a fair share of criticism as well.

The currencies' rapid rise and their uncertain legal status has led some investors and lawmakers to warn of potential scams or market manipulation.

At the same time, authorities in a number of countries have taken a close look at cryptocurrencies, including China, India, the UK, South Korea, Japan, and the US.

New York state's Department of Financial Services, for instance, is exploring a number of options for regulating digital currencies.

In Malaysia, central bank deputy governor Datuk Koh Sung-wha has warned against the risks of investing in cryptocurrencies, saying the virtual currencies had shown a tendency to see their values rise too quickly and their underlying assets did not necessarily hold real value.

China, home to many of the world's leading cryptocurrency players, has banned financial institutions from trading in cryptocurrencies, and announced that it was banning initial coin offerings -- a practice in which start-up companies issue virtual coins or tokens, which can be bought and sold like stocks -- from September.

And the US Securities and Exchange Commission is currently investigating cryptocurrency price manipulation.

As a result, a number of financial companies, including Goldman Sachs, have stopped directly dealing in bitcoin.

Why are the currencies surging now?

Analysts are of the view that the recent price spike was driven by increased interest from retail investors and institutional investors, due to increased speculation on their future value, as well as growing acceptance by retailers.

Additionally, more developers are contributing to blockchain technology and this, in turn, is making the technology more robust and popular.

"The blockchain is the essential technology that enables bitcoin and a number of other cryptocurrencies to function as distributed ledgers, which makes it difficult to tamper with the records and prevent forgery," says Nisha Gopalan, the cofounder of Calypso, a fintech start-up that has developed a blockchain-based system for the Malaysian ringgit.

"As the blockchain moves closer to mass market adoption, investors have more confidence in cryptocurrencies, which has increased the value of cryptocurrencies."

Blockchain, which powers cryptocurrencies, is a decentralized database that acts like a shared diary for all the transactions made on a cryptocurrency network.

"Blockchain is transparent and secure and as more developers learn about it, it becomes increasingly more widely used. Since most retailers accept bitcoin, this drives up its value," says Gopalan.

In Malaysia, the central bank has not moved to halt bitcoin transactions, unlike in many other countries, including China, where the use of digital currencies is banned.

Instead, the central bank has asked its member banks to conduct risk assessment studies on digital currencies to ascertain their risks and vulnerabilities.

Malaysia's central bank has established a committee to study the existing regulatory framework for virtual currencies, and to assess if additional laws and regulations are needed.

Malaysia's finance minister said in March that cryptocurrency trading should be regulated, but did not specify whether he wanted to ban it or introduce stricter regulations.

In Singapore, where cryptocurrency trading is also unregulated, the central bank has issued two public warnings over the past few months.

In October, it said that investors should exercise "extreme

caution" when trading in the cryptocurrency, while in November it issued a warning that trading in digital currencies had become highly speculative.

In its latest report, the Monetary Authority of Singapore said that bitcoin is not a currency or an asset, but is more of a "crypto-asset" that, while created through cryptographically secure cryptography, lacks the legal or economic backing of any nation-state.

History of Bitcoin.

Bitcoin is a peer to peer network that has no central authority to regulate transactions or issue currency. Instead, each wallet and node has its own copy of the bitcoin ledger, which acts as a public, global ledger that is synchronized across all computers and devices that communicate with each other.

Per the Blockchain, the first peer to peer electronic cash system, "Every bitcoin transaction is recorded in a log called the Blockchain. Every 10 minutes, the Blockchain is updated to record and record all past transactions." The Blockchain is publicly viewable by anyone with access to the Internet. The Blockchain records not only purchases and sales but every single transaction made on the network. Bitcoin is open source, free, secure and scalable. Bitcoin does not require a central authority to process or track transactions.

Bitcoin utilizes a "proof of work" method for confirming and tracking transactions. The system works as follows. A total number of Bitcoins are created in predetermined increments of 25 bitcoins every ten minutes. To validate a transaction, a certain number of bitcoins are required to make the payment. The public ledger of transactions that shows the transaction, the sender and receiver as well as the amount are required. A private key that can be used to spend the bitcoins is required.

There are 21 million bitcoins, and once all Bitcoins have been mined or used for transactions, the remaining bitcoins can never be created again. Bitcoin users can purchase the digital currency using Bitcoins. Users can purchase Bitcoins using local exchanges or they can purchase Bitcoins on online exchanges. Each Bitcoin is assigned a unique key known as a public key and a private key, which are used to track and control the electronic funds.

Digital money versus traditional money

Bitcoin and other alternative currencies are digital and work as a distributed ledger system which removes the possibility of government or centralized authority as a means of storing and moving or regulating digital currency. Bitcoins, Litecoins and Dogecoin are digital forms of currency that function on the Bitcoin blockchain system.

Because of Bitcoin and other alternative forms of money, the business world is now looking into this system. If you buy a coffee for 5 dollars and pay with a plastic or real currency, that transaction is recorded and recorded at every merchant in the country, which can be traced back to your account. This system is called the monetary system. This system operates with a bank, therefore, the government is involved. Using a system such as Bitcoin, which is a decentralized system that does not allow the government or bank to regulate the transactions and uses cryptography, the government does not know who you are, or which physical location the payment was made. In other words, the government cannot trace a transaction.

Bitcoin and other alternative forms of money represent new economic challenges for the global economic system and its central banks. Most governments are against Bitcoin as an alternative currency because they feel it undermines their power and monetary system. However, Bitcoin has established itself as an alternative currency with many advantages. If governments and central banks allow their control over and regulation of money to be replaced with alternative forms of money that operate outside of the control of a government or central bank, there is a potential loss of power and a revolution for independence. Some may call this centralized power run out of control. In the United States, Bitcoin is recognized as a means of payment and a digital currency. A Department of Homeland Security official has compared Bitcoin with dollars. Some refer to Bitcoin as the new gold.

However, Bitcoin is not recognized by the Federal Reserve or the Federal Deposit Insurance Corp. It also has an exchange rate disadvantage compared to other currencies. You can convert an Italian lira into US dollars at 1:1 or worse. Conversely, you can convert bitcoins into dollars at 1:16 or worse. It is a difficult currency to convert. You also do not have access to a bank account. Bitcoin is also not regulated by any government or central bank. The Bitcoin system is still very much in its infancy. It has some weaknesses and there is not enough time to address the shortcomings as we currently stand. The future is bright for Bitcoin, but it has a long way to go.

If governments and central banks allow their control over and regulation of money to be replaced with alternative forms of money that operate outside of the control of a government or central bank, there is a potential loss of power and a revolution for independence.

How to exchange Cryptocurrencies?

There are many exchanges that you can use in the market to exchange Cryptocurrencies and the process is very easy and simple.

Here is the quick overview about the exchange process and you can easily exchange Cryptocurrencies.

Find a reliable exchange that matches your money and keep in mind that you should make sure the exchange you chose is providing you the best exchange rates.

Here is the information about coins and base rate:

Any good exchange will provide you coins based on the market standard. We are not going to make you pay for the base rate. The value of Bitcoin is just one of the important factors you should consider while making an exchange.

Buy and sell Bitcoins: The market standard is worth 0.5% of the coin (e.g. $250 for Bitcoin $10,000 is equal to $24000 for the price of Bitcoin $1000).

1% for all other Cryptocurrencies such as Ethereum, Litecoin, Ripple etc.

1% for the trading fees

If you find an exchange that offers you the maximum possible amount of coins, that is awesome, you can buy Bitcoins and buy other cryptocurrency, then you need to see if that exchange is reputable and follow the usual things listed above.

Do not use an exchange that offers you less coins or base rate.

Choose an exchange that offers you coin base rate and coin buying base rate. It means that if you buy Bitcoins at 1% base rate and you want to buy other cryptocurrency, you should exchange that coin to 0.5% or 0.25% coin base rate. So you should buy Bitcoins at 1% and other cryptocurrency at 0.5% or 0.25%. So you should use a Bitcoin buying exchange that offers you a coin buying rate as well as coin base rate.

That is all about buying and selling cryptocurrencies. If you want to learn more about cryptocurrency trading you can check out our page that explains the basics of trading.

Chapter 3 Cryptocurrency trading

How to exchange Cryptocurrencies?

Transferring Cryptocurrencies to a friend or to another cryptocurrency user is generally as simple as sending them coins. However, when you go to send coins to your friend, you may have to clarify to them what kind of coins you are trying to transfer.

Most of the exchanges have the necessary filters to verify the sender and the receiver. Once you have set this, your recipient can now receive the coins as if they were receiving it from a friend who has the same address. The recipient can even redeem the coins on a mobile application, but that's up to them.

When you transfer coins from one exchange to another, you can only send the coins as cash, which is to be converted to the platform that you are transferring. This means that you have to convert the coins from the exchange to your own crypto wallet, and vice versa. If you are transferring it from a platform to another exchange, it is referred to as a double conversion.

Alternatively, you can exchange them on a mobile application, which has a built-in exchange. When you buy and sell tokens or cryptocurrencies on the platform, the conversion is automatic.

So, cryptocurrency exchange, trading, or lending are very different from fiat currency exchanges. They work differently with some of them having an ideal role for those who wish to convert the cryptocurrency to their currency of choice. On the other hand, some of them are a crucial part of the whole ecosystem for those wishing to use the cryptocurrency in their everyday lives, and those looking to make an investment of any type.

Where to exchange cryptocurrencies?

There are many exchanges in the world and all of them have their own technicalities and offer their own trading features. Which means there's no "default exchange" for bitcoins or any other cryptocurrency in the world. It's a bit difficult for an outsider to know which exchange is better than another, given all the rules, regulations and constantly changing technicalities involved. If you want to make an exchange with cryptocurrencies you should go into business with a business partner. That is the only way you can have better access to information on all exchanges and trust each other. It might be worth talking to a professional bitcoin and bitcoin cash trader to get advice about all the potential risks and pitfalls that a bitcoin trader should know before participating in the market.

Some of the exchanges are not regulated at all, some require users to show a phone number and user ID to register. And some of the exchanges provide KYC details that some even require to link all your bank accounts.

How to find and trade your coins in the cryptocurrency market?

We believe trading cryptocurrencies can be very rewarding, but you have to understand that you are dealing with something which is not regulated, the entire ecosystem is moving fast and you should not judge your trade by your own ability to calculate risk. Just remember, cryptocurrency is not the same as ordinary currency. You should be ready to lose a lot of money if the coin you are trading is not in the right price range at the right moment, so understand that.

But there are many other factors that you should consider when entering the market:

Convenience is important

A lot of people want to trade cryptocurrencies, but they are not able to take the time to switch between exchanges, download the app and login with their social accounts in order to make a transaction. That is why they ask for a good market with one good exchange where they can move their coins and be able to take advantage of all the benefits associated with cryptocurrency trading.

A lot of the coins have a "Fork Problem"

Some coins are forked from the original Bitcoin software. This means that a significant part of the development community of the original bitcoin didn't like the way they were developing it and they decided to fork the software. The new coins are called Bitcoin Cash, Bitcoin Gold, Bitcoin Silver etc. Sometimes users decide to trade one coin for another and to do that they need to send their coins to another exchange in order to trade one cryptocurrency for another. In this case, there's a risk of sending your coins to a second exchange which you are not aware of and which might be a scam. Be cautious, make sure that you know who you are trading with and only send your coins to exchange addresses that you trust.

Security is key

Unfortunately, the security of cryptocurrencies is still quite new and not all exchanges have the same level of security. In order to be safe, be sure to watch out for unexpected charges, scammers and issues with your account (it happens a lot). Here are some great steps you can follow:

Register with exchanges

Open a separate account in order to transfer your coins to exchanges. This way you can control your assets in order to protect them from scammers and at the same time, you are guaranteed that no one else will have access to them. You can create an account in any of the exchanges listed above. Don't put all your eggs in one basket!

Research a lot before you invest

Before you make a transaction, you should research a bit about the coin or the exchange where you want to buy/sell your cryptocurrency. You should try to get as much information about the exchange and the coins available on the exchange as possible. It is recommended to set a budget that you are willing to risk, but be aware that cryptocurrency prices are constantly changing and sometimes they change more quickly than you can handle. You might be tempted to make a quick transaction, which can turn out to be expensive if the cryptocurrency price goes up or down. Be careful, don't trade too often and always double check your statements.

Invest with a reputable exchange

Check the reputation of the exchange. There are many sites which rate the exchange with a 1 to 10 scale. Don't trust just any average rating. In addition, be sure that the exchange you are trading with is registered and based in a good jurisdiction. When it comes to security, most exchanges offer a feature called multisignature where you can specify the number of keys that are needed to make a transaction. Make sure you read the entire privacy policy of the exchange and the terms and conditions (T&C) as well. The information disclosed in the T&C of the exchange can lead to a violation of your privacy. You should be aware of the implications of working with a suspicious exchange.

Don't go it alone

You might be tempted to exchange your money on your own. If you decide to do it, make sure you know how you'll send your money to the exchange and who will receive your money. If you don't understand the steps of the process, you will probably send your coins to a fake exchange. This is why it's essential to use a professional broker. You can find brokers on CoinOutlet, Changelly or Coinapult and you can learn more about them here.

Does this sound complicated? Not really. But make sure you understand everything about cryptocurrency before you invest. Don't be afraid to ask questions to your broker or other experienced users. After all, you're making a big decision and the potential to lose your money is very real.

Make sure that you use a safe and secure platform, but make sure you don't forget to share this article with someone who is not familiar with cryptocurrencies. This way you'll be able to avoid a disaster like losing all your coins. If you did your research well, all you have to do is forget your password and start trading. Don't risk it on a random website.

How to start cryptocurrency trading?

Starting off with cryptocurrency trading might be easy but turning a profit in such a volatile market might be a difficult task. This is where a good trading platform comes in. This will show you the best and cheapest way to trade cryptocurrencies like Bitcoin and others in a fast, efficient, and smooth way.

What are the benefits of a cryptocurrency trading platform?

When you're going into a new market, it takes a bit of trust and research to decide whether or not to invest in it. However, if you're going into trading and investing in cryptocurrency, then you should go with a reputable cryptocurrency trading platform that has loads of resources and tutorials to get you up to speed quickly. They will make your journey easier and make sure you make the right decisions.

What are the disadvantages of a cryptocurrency trading platform?

To trade with cryptocurrencies, you need a good platform that will not only guide you through the process, but will also provide you with every possible resource and the best practice of such an activity. This can take a lot of time to research and make sure everything is in place and works as it should. This is why using a reputable platform is very important, as this is where you'll find information and they will guide you step by step as you make your choice and start trading.

How can you find the right platform to start with?

There are many different ways to do this. You can either research the cryptocurrency trading platforms or visit different forums and groups to see what is available. While there are some really good crypto communities, there are some that are much more active and won't hesitate to ask any question that they may have. There are also different forums and groups that have a lot of members that might be willing to help you out.

These exchanges and trading platforms are great ways to start trading with cryptocurrencies but it can take some time to start. You need to decide what currencies to invest in and how to buy them. This is very important and you should make sure to have an idea of which currencies to trade and the steps needed to do it.

There are also different places where you can trade and invest in cryptocurrencies. You need to be careful when you choose your place to trade and invest in cryptocurrency, so you don't get into any trouble.

However, with a good trading and investing platform, your journey will be a lot smoother and easier and it can take you a lot less time to make money in cryptocurrency.

Where to Start?

If you want to make money in cryptocurrency you can start by going to a good trading and investing platform. In fact, there are several platforms out there and each one comes with its own advantages and disadvantages.

Cryptocurrency is a bit of a niche market. If you're not very familiar with trading and investing in cryptocurrencies, then you'll need to find the best platform to start trading and investing in cryptocurrency.

How to Choose The Right Cryptocurrency Trading

Platform

1. Take Your Time

You need to take your time when selecting a reputable cryptocurrency trading and investing platform. Take the time to research the different platforms and decide which ones you think will help you the most. This will make the entire process easier for you and you can start trading and investing in cryptocurrency as soon as you have made your choice.

2. Choose Cryptocurrency Trading Platforms With a Good Reputation

This is one of the most important things you need to remember. Your choice of cryptocurrency trading platform is a choice that will shape your entire experience in cryptocurrency. Therefore, you need to choose a cryptocurrency trading platform that has a reputation that is able to back up the information it provides.

This is important. A bad reputation and exchange with an unclear trading system or market position can lead to you losing a lot of money. While some platforms might have good reputations, this doesn't mean all of them will.

3. Check out Trading Metrics

Before you decide which trading platform to use, you need to take some time to read the different trading metrics. This is important because this will help you to understand how to evaluate and gauge the platform in order to see whether it can help you get the best returns.

You can see the exchange that looks good by checking out its different metrics such as the volume and market trends. You can also take a look at how long it takes to complete a trade and how quickly it reaches your trader account.

4. If It's A Good Cryptocurrency Trading Platform, It Will Help You With Profitability

With a good trading platform, you will be able to achieve high profits and in the long term. However, you should always consider the risk involved with cryptocurrency trading before you make any final decision.

5. Look for Cryptocurrency Trading Platforms with Cryptocurrency Exchanges

Most platforms offer an exchange where you can trade with other users. Make sure you choose the right exchange for your cryptocurrency. Don't choose a platform that doesn't allow you to trade.

6. Look for Multiple Cryptocurrency Exchanges

You can choose a single cryptocurrency exchange or you can choose several cryptocurrencies. Usually, multiple cryptocurrency exchanges are better. For example, you can choose exchanges that have high volume or liquidity. If this is the case, then you will be able to make money a lot faster and more efficiently.

7. Choose An Exchange That's Supported By a Wide Range of Cryptocurrencies

This is very important. If the exchange has a high volume of cryptocurrency trading, then it's likely to be used by many people, and this will make it easier for you to achieve high profits. In order to make money in cryptocurrency trading, you need to choose an exchange that has a lot of liquidity in order to support your cryptocurrency trades.

8. Take Your Time and Make Your Choices

There is no hard-and-fast rule to picking a cryptocurrency trading and investing platform. Make your decision and then make sure to let the platform test your luck before you make any final decision.

Chapter 4 How to read trading graphs?

Trading analysis is a specialized branch of mathematics or applied mathematics. Since the analysis has no direct application in the real world, graphs or charts provide an abstraction, to show patterns, trends and risks.

Computing is a branch of mathematics or applied mathematics. In the past it was not possible to have programs that used cryptography, such as RSA, where many (known) numbers are kept secret. But now we have the computers.

So a problem for computers and for software is how to show what was happening for a particular time and for particular amounts in particular markets.

Trading is often depicted with charts, and one can therefore see what's been happening, in a way similar to a bar chart. However there are several key differences, and there are also some important differences between charts and graphs, but that's a problem for another post.

To illustrate trading terms and levels, here is a simplified example of a trading graph:

The market is represented by the red line in the chart. The position of a trader, represented by the blue circle, is a range-bound buy/sell, and is subject to external factors (trading news, news from outside the game). The strategy is buy at price x, sell at price y.

The trading-gap (shown by the green box on the left) is the difference between the current price and the average price in the past. For a normal buy/sell strategy, the gap is large.

However this particular range-bound buy/sell position has very low trading-gap, because the position is limited by the numbers (100 at best). This means that the position is often in a 'no-man's land', which is known as a dead zone.

This is one of the primary use-cases of trading graphs: to show the underlying pattern of a trade that was perhaps in a dead zone. This type of graph is not likely to provide insight into the "big picture" of the market, but it could be useful to show trends, or to suggest a level to watch.

In some sense, each point (in the graph) represents a trade, which is shown in an interesting way with a thicker color. For a given point, if you trace a line from that point to the next, it shows how far the trade spread (how far the price changed during a trade).

Trading graphs can be broken into 3 main categories:

Dashed lines

Trading patterns are commonly represented with a dashed line, with the current price in the vertical axis and the average price in the horizontal axis. The point of the line is the current price, and the unit of measurement is called the scale of price (from very high to very low).

Using this type of graph, you can see whether a trade "caught the market" (liked the trade), or whether it "sailed away" (dodged the market), or whether it "chased the market" (chased the next most liquid trade).

Dashed line trading is useful because it's easy to show a period (spanning several days) and shows the relative size of the spread between the current price and the average price.

Dashed lines are also quite common on high-frequency trading (HFT) screens, but they're often replaced with a line that's often not as easily understandable (and often less relevant).

Two popular types of charts with a line are candlestick charts and WMA charts.

On candlestick charts, the high/low data is usually shown in a chart that goes up and down, with price at the top and bottom. On WMA charts, instead, the high/low data is shown in a box with a long slope, that rises and falls at a smooth angle.

The advantage of this type of chart is that the whole chart often looks alike. However this is both a disadvantage and an advantage, depending on what you're looking at.

The advantage is that it's easy to see the trading flow for a period of time (perhaps 2 or 3 days), whereas it's much harder to do this with WMA charts.

The disadvantage is that the long slope makes the line look like an S, and makes it harder to see the period. Also, it's harder to measure, because you can't see the current price.

Once you think you're a bit closer to the trading data, you can see that it's more appropriate to use a WMA chart, or a straight line.

Stacked lines

Trading patterns are typically shown as a stacked bar chart, with the current price in the first bar, the average price in the second bar, and the price of each individual trade in the third bar.

If you look closely, you'll see that many of these trading patterns look similar to a WMA chart, but this can be useful for those who can see the trading data more easily.

The benefit of this type of chart is that it makes the price of each individual trade visible, instead of showing the whole chart.

The disadvantage is that it can be hard to see the trading data, and if you have a HFT screen (which usually only has one or two lines in your graph), it's hard to find any significant action.

The three bar type is the most common, and is also a "dashed line" chart. It's the most commonly used type of chart on high-frequency trading screens, but you can use it for other purposes.

By default, it has three bars, representing the current price, the average price, and the price of each individual trade.

This is very similar to an HFT chart, but with three bars representing the current price, the average price, and the price of each individual trade.

To change the number of bars, you'll need to switch to "Line options" on your chart settings.

Quad line charts

Another popular, more straightforward, way of displaying a trading pattern is to use a quad chart.

This type of chart has four horizontal bars (shown in yellow), representing the average price of each individual trade.

This chart is frequently used on HFT screens.

Quad charts are a good way of quickly comparing trading patterns, but they're not necessarily as good for all chart types.

They're much better for making patterns visible on a bigger

chart than for displaying trading activity on a line chart.

Note: if you switch to "Line options" you can choose "Stacked" instead of "Quad".

Bar-and-line charts

Bar-and-line charts are a simplified version of the famous "golden spiral" chart, where each line represents a single trade.

The advantage of this chart is that it uses a classic geometric shape, rather than simply showing bars of different lengths.

The disadvantage is that it's hard to read the movement of the data because the pattern has four straight lines.

This chart might be useful for making a trading pattern clear from a smaller graph.

Variations on the horizontal bar chart

Another popular form of trading pattern is a horizontal bar chart, with each line representing a different day, and not all at the same time.

The disadvantage of this type of chart is that, although it's great for showing a big range of trading patterns, it's not very effective at showing any one pattern.

This is usually shown in HFT screens, but sometimes it's used elsewhere, for example, in a breakout chart, or if there's not enough data to create a "golden spiral".

One-dimensional charts

As well as the quad and bar charts mentioned above, you can also create a one-dimensional trading pattern. This will usually use the same two pieces of data to show the pattern, but will show it on just one line.

You'll usually see this type of pattern used on low-frequency trading screens.

You'll be able to see it as a thin horizontal line, with each line representing one day. It doesn't look like much, but when you overlay this type of chart with a quad chart, you can see all the trading activity for that day:

You can use the horizontal bar chart as a one-dimensional trading pattern, but you'll need to put the bars in different colours to show the full pattern. You'll need to either choose "one line" for each bar, or switch to "Line options", if you're using the vertical bar chart.

Another good one-dimensional chart, especially for smaller trades, is a "half time chart".

This will show a single trading period from beginning to end, but with only one pattern.

You can see the first few trading periods using this type of chart. As the pattern progresses, the bars will start to move together.

There are variations on the half time chart, too. For example, you can have the bars in "melts", which show the trading period as a whole.

Why do trading patterns disappear?

If you're keen to learn more about how trading patterns are displayed, take a look at this free video:

You may also be wondering why certain trading patterns disappear.

This is because they're supposed to. It means that there's nothing of value that can be learned by studying them.

For example, the next chart shows a simple trading pattern, and you can see that there's nothing in the patterns for the first day and the third day.

This means there's no need to analyse the first two days of trading activity:

It might be interesting to know that on the third day, one trade traded at twice the previous day's price, but there's no need to know why this happened, because you can't work out anything useful from this pattern.

How trading patterns work

So, now you've seen how trading patterns work, what's the point?

Trading patterns can show the changing behaviour of the stock price over time, which is the main reason people use them in their trading systems.

Trading patterns can also tell you when a stock price is likely to move, whether it's because a major event is coming, or it's already happened. This is useful for you to know in advance, and for others, so you can time their trading activity to take advantage of the event, and not to be caught on the wrong side of it.

Trading patterns can help you spot trends, which is another important reason to use them.

A pattern for a specific trading period can also give you an idea of whether a stock price has "bottomed out".

This is important, because once a stock price has "bottomed out", it's often seen as a good value to start to build a long position in it. It means that the stock price is likely to rise in the future.

You can see that on the third day, the price briefly dropped from $18 to $15. But the pattern revealed that the price would soon recover.

Of course, the way that a trading pattern works is that you need to pay attention to it. For example, when a trading pattern breaks, it means that something has happened.

This doesn't mean you should be completely cynical and assume this is a "market-tracker" selling at a loss to make room for more profit. Rather, it means you should analyse what this pattern means, and use this information to make an informed trading decision.

For example, if a pattern says that a stock price is likely to fall to a certain level before it starts to recover, you can start to build a short position at that level.

What is a relative strength index?

A high relative strength index indicates that an asset is outperforming another asset. A low relative strength index, on the other hand, means that the asset is underperforming.

How is relative strength calculated?

The relative strength index is calculated by taking the standard deviation of an asset's price movements and dividing that by the standard deviation of all prices.

Which markets are the strongest?

In October 2017, the S&P 500 index outperformed the S&P GSCI index by a large margin. In March 2018, the S&P GSCI outperformed the S&P 500 by a smaller margin, with the two indexes showing minimal net outflows for the period.

When are relative strength indices most helpful?

An investment professional needs to know what the market is saying about the fundamentals of a specific company or security, not the overall market, so a relative strength index can be a useful tool to help tell that story. A number of strategies in a portfolio will use relative strength to their advantage.

Chapter 5 How to make the technical analysis of trading?

The best resource which can be used to identify the bitcoin price is the bitcointrends.com, which is constantly updated with the technical analysis for different exchanges. In particular, they track the Chinese bitcoin price in particular and give a lot of information about it.

There is also a very useful bitcoin ticker for trading tips which can be found at bitcointradingtips.com. It is very popular on social networks and has a great following.

What is the difference between the CFD and the CFD position?

Before entering the market you need to know more about the difference between the CFD and the CFD position. The traditional one is a contract for difference (CFD). This means that you deposit a fixed amount of money to place a bet with the market at your desired price. You know the price you are betting for, but not the profit you will make if the price goes up or down.

The CFD position is ideal for people who know what they want to buy and what they are trying to buy it for. If you buy a block you need to use a certain amount of money, not a random amount of money. That means you need to place a larger bet and profit more if the price goes up.

The CFD position is an ideal way to learn about bitcoin. It is for everyone who wants to get a small amount of money to experiment, but doesn't want to have to risk too much if they lose it.

What is the size of an actual order in CFD vs. spread?

There is a great exchange called London Block Exchange, which has the most bitcoins trading per second, compared to many other platforms. They offer 0.0025 BTC per market as a minimum trade. Other larger and safer platforms such as Bitfinex and Bitmex offer 0.01 BTC per market as a minimum trade.

CFD spreads are also commonly traded, which is good if you don't have much money to place a large bet, but otherwise it's better to choose the CFD option.

Why should I use a spread?

In case you have a lot of money, it can be tempting to simply enter an order and then immediately place a sell or buy order, which in this case means placing the first order 0.0025 BTC, and then 0.01 BTC.

This way, you don't need to wait the full 24 hours to place a buy or sell order and if the price changes, you can immediately enter another trade. It's called a spread because you are placing a sell order on one currency, while a buy order on another. Usually, you're getting a good spread that provides the opportunity to profit.

For example, if you buy 200 bitcoins for 0.01 BTC, and then sell them for 0.02 BTC, you have a 0.04 BTC profit. If the price at the time of your sell order is higher, and the price at the time of your buy order is lower, you have a profit of 0.04 bitcoin.

If you don't want to do it that way, the standard is to place a trade of 0.01 BTC for each market. In this case, you will have a total of 0.01 BTC, you can then buy or sell on each market. The result is a total profit of 0.01 bitcoin for each market.

Do you need to understand what a BitStamp is?

In most cases, if you buy a lot of bitcoins on one exchange, you won't need to understand the value, why its value has changed, and where it is now. It is common to sell large amounts of bitcoins at a certain period of time.

For example, if you have a big order, and the price on that market is going up, you can always enter a smaller trade, so the order won't go through at the same time as your large order. This way you can maximize your profits.

What are the fees if you use a spreads?

If you choose to go with spreads, your fees will be higher. Some markets charge an extra 0.10-0.12 per order.

On the bigger exchanges, you might even need to pay the spread fee, which could be between 0.01 BTC and 0.07 BTC.

What is the fee if you use the CFD with USD?

If you want to make a deposit with USD, you can avoid the spread fee. It will be a fixed fee that ranges between 0.04-0.06 depending on the market.

What is the fee if you want to use the euro?

On the bigger exchanges, the spreads cost 0.04-0.06, but you can avoid the spread fee by using a leverage option. For example, if you buy 100 bitcoins for 0.01 BTC, you can buy another 100 bitcoins for 0.01 BTC, and then buy another 100 bitcoins for 0.01 BTC. This way the market would actually balance, you wouldn't be able to profit on the first 100 bitcoins.

What are supports and resistances in trading?

Trading is inherently a balancing act between the forces of supply and demand. Although the markets are relatively free, there are many barriers that prevent a simple trade to go the way it is supposed to go. What is known as the "price discovery" of the market, the search for the best price for a product or service, takes place in the market with a certain level of confidence in the presence of buyers and sellers. The strategy of market-makers, the entities or companies that initiate and execute orders in the market to set a price, is to determine that price by using a feedback mechanism that allows them to figure out the distribution of current and future interests on the part of buyers and sellers.

The three most commonly used feedback mechanisms in the market are called "anchors", "curves" and "histograms".

Anchor

This feedback mechanism looks for a price that has a high degree of support and low degree of resistance.

The simplest anchor system is the first. There is only one point in the market that is used for reference, but it is enough to know that you don't want to trade there because it is only supported by a very small percent of the market.

The second version of an anchor system is the simple differential, which is a price difference based on different rates of change. This price is supported by a greater than 90 percent of the market, because at least 90 percent of buyers are willing to pay that price difference. This price is also supported by a much lower than 0 percent of the market because a small number of sellers are willing to accept that price difference for their goods.

The final version of an anchor system is the historical differential, which is a price difference based on a number of different prices. In other words, the price of an item is shown against a number of different reference prices.

Curve

The curve strategy looks for a price that is likely to have a future development consistent with a specified expectation. This price is supported by a higher degree of support and a lower level of resistance than an anchor system, but it is still a little bit more expensive than an anchor system.

Curves can take many forms, but they have a few important characteristics. First, they are usually rather narrow. Second, they may be connected to other price moves. Third, they tend to occur as small deviations from the fundamental value of the market.

Histogram

The histogram system involves searching for a set of points that is close to a unique value. The narrow size of the price range that the system is able to trade within is very important.

What is a technical analysis system?

The original technical analysis was the W-o-W system, which is used in the commodity trading markets to help the broker to determine a price target for a trade. The price target is the maximum that the commodity could possibly go without becoming unprofitable. An example would be the price of wheat could go up to $5.30, but a broker would consider it unprofitable to sell that wheat below $5.05.

The W-o-W system goes further to determine the potential targets for a trade. The price ranges within a given price range are the most promising targets.

The W-o-W model can be used on either a daily or a monthly time scale. The monthly time scale is preferred because it provides much more flexibility and ease in integrating the past price changes and future developments.

It should be noted that there are other fundamental or technical systems that are used for technical analysis. However, these are used with a much broader range of assets and prices than the W-o-W model.

The basic strategy is to create an entry and a potential exit price range for the trade. It is also necessary to determine the entry level and the potential exit level of the trade. This is done by adjusting the "prices" of the W-o-W model against the different trade ranges to determine the entry and potential exit prices.

A simple example is shown in Figure 1. The exchange rate between the Canadian dollar and the United States dollar is the basis for the basis for the trade. The open and close prices are the basis for the price. The exchange rate between the U.S. dollar and the Chinese renminbi is the basis for the price of the trade. The price for the basis is the basis. The weight and the volume of the open and close prices are the basis and volume for the price. In other words, the R-value represents the number of dollars that can be traded with a single U.S. dollar.

By looking at the basis and the price, the length of the position can be calculated.

Here is what happens if we close at $1.086. We make money if we are at the entry price and at the potential exit price. This will be the volume, or the trading price, for the total dollar amount of the position.

If we close at $1.086, we would make money if we were at the entry price and at the potential exit price.

If we were at $1.086 at $1.0731, then we would make money at the possibility that we are at the $1.086 entry price and the possibility that we are at the $1.0731 entry price.

Now we must consider the potential range of the price action. The black line is the potential range of the price of the trade and the solid red line is the price. A trade from $1.086 to $1.0731 will be a black point. A trade from $1.086 to $1.0731 will be a red point.

The risk of a trade is the spread that must be made over the potential ranges. The dotted green line shows the risk of the trade if the trade is held for a period of one day. The green box shows the risk of the trade if the trade is held for one week. The black box shows the risk of the trade if the trade is held for two weeks.

73

Chapter 6 How to save cryptocurrency?

How to protect cryptocurrency?

Blockchain technology is supposed to be secure. That's one reason it is so widely used in Bitcoin and other cryptocurrencies. They are digital assets that you own only because you have proof of ownership. These are not like stocks or bonds or even mutual funds.

When you trade these digital assets, you exchange them for some form of currency, like dollars, pounds, euros or yuan. The amount of currency you can exchange is determined by how many coins are in your wallet. If you sell or trade these assets, you can buy back some of them from other traders. And, if you lose or destroy your wallet, you can't get new ones.

That makes them much less volatile than the currencies and assets most people hold. They are "tied up" with you, a person with a public and easily traceable identity.

The worst that could happen with a cryptocurrency is that you lost the coins. But if you are rich enough to be immune to that risk, you can be pretty much indifferent to losing the money. If you are less wealthy and therefore have a lot to lose, it is much more dangerous.

Many people are currently using Bitcoin to buy drugs, as was recently revealed in a New York Times exposé. They may also be using it to move their money out of other countries where regulations, taxation, or both make it difficult to move money around.

Governments around the world are starting to move against Bitcoin. Most recently, the U.K. government told online Bitcoin exchanges that they would no longer be allowed to accept deposits from customers in the United Kingdom. And, this past April, China outlawed Bitcoin exchanges entirely. But Bitcoin is not going away.

Should you invest in it?

But, there are reasons you might want to buy Bitcoin. Maybe you want to protect your Bitcoin investments against the possible consequences of a severe economic crisis. Or you might want to leverage that money into more valuable assets like stocks, real estate or gold.

Other investors might simply want to speculate on future Bitcoin price movements. And there is evidence that a lot of speculators do not do much research about the investments they're making. Some people buy Bitcoin without bothering to learn much about the currency, much less how to buy or sell it.

Those kinds of people are the reason why Bitcoin has seen a

huge rise in value and volatility recently, even as government crackdowns and negative news stories have increased.

Are cryptocurrency bubbles just bubbles?

It's worth noting that many stock market bubbles have also been "created" by people trading or speculating on relatively illiquid assets. The tulip mania of the early 17th century is perhaps the best-known of these bubbles.

Many of the people who invested in tulip bulbs were also speculators. And some people who bought or traded in tulip bulbs also suffered big losses. But no matter how quickly those speculators were buying or selling, the value of those bulbs couldn't fall very quickly. So, it was very easy for them to lose a lot of money — perhaps up to a hundred times what they originally paid for the bulbs.

Investors who are trying to time the market — buying and selling shares when a stock price is low and vice versa — have a much harder time keeping their losses down. That's because market participants don't always react in the same way to the same news, even when the news is in the same direction.

In early April, the price of one Bitcoin was $2,000. By May 9, it was $5,000. Other Bitcoin prices also rose sharply, but that's not why most people rushed to buy Bitcoin. They were speculators, taking advantage of price increases to make some fast money before the price fell back.

Can the price keep rising?

It may seem tempting to think that Bitcoin's price will keep rising, but there are two main reasons why that's unlikely to happen.

First, there are Bitcoin "miners," who use massive computers to solve complex math problems in order to add new Bitcoin to the network. In exchange for computing the math problems, miners get new Bitcoin as a reward.

The miners can't make more Bitcoin unless they also make more electricity to run their computers. So, the more machines they have running, the less incentive there is for them to keep up the pace of adding new Bitcoin.

Even after the sharp price increase of the past few months, Bitcoin miners only have 17,000 more Bitcoin to go before they run out of what's needed to keep their computers running. That would take them roughly 14 years.

But, with mining increasingly unable to meet demand, and the number of machines currently running almost at its limit, it's unlikely that anyone will be able to dramatically increase the Bitcoin supply any time soon.

It's likely that the number of Bitcoin miners will decline over time, which would eventually slow down the creation of new Bitcoin. That would lower the price, which might create the risk of another "bubble" like the one we saw in April.

Of course, it's possible that the number of miners could decline by a huge amount without triggering a crash in the price. Bitcoin's developers could agree to release a large amount of new currency at once, which would allow miners to keep working with less effort.

But that may not happen — there are competing visions of how Bitcoin should work, and the developers may not come to an agreement.

Second, the market for Bitcoin is very small — far smaller than the number of computers that are needed to mine the currency. That means a sudden crash in demand could make it difficult for miners to keep working — even if the price of Bitcoin falls.

In other words, even if miners keep up their pace of producing new Bitcoin, new computer power isn't enough to prevent a future crash in the price. That's why experts like Daniele Bianchi, a professor at the Warwick Business School, say that the chances of a bubble bursting are now about the same as those of the dot-com bubble.

Is this what will happen?

It's impossible to say for sure how the Bitcoin market will behave. There's always the chance that the network will add a lot more new Bitcoin without triggering another crash. It may start making new Bitcoins relatively quickly, or it may take longer.

So, it's possible that there will be another Bitcoin bubble. But at this point, it looks unlikely.

But as with all financial markets, if I was looking for an investment that would provide big profits even if the price of Bitcoin kept rising, I'd go with something else.

So, where is Bitcoin making money right now?

Well, you can buy Bitcoin directly — or you can mine it if you have the proper equipment — but you won't get very much value from doing either one.

A few years ago, Bitcoin was still a relatively niche market. But lately, there's been a significant increase in interest — and that's meant a big rise in the value of the digital currency.

That's mostly driven by a surge in interest from mainstream investors, who see the virtual currency as an alternative to "paper" currencies like the US dollar.

But some of the price increase is because Bitcoin has been becoming more attractive for people who want to make online payments, or to run "mines."

These are people who are willing to let their computers work continuously for months or years, if they can get paid for the work with Bitcoins.

One of the big issues with Bitcoin was that most people couldn't mine the currency — or didn't have the right equipment. These days, you can run a Bitcoin "mine" using a standard PC.

The supply of Bitcoins is limited, so if too many people start mining, the currency would start falling in value. That's why the "mining" of Bitcoin is currently slowing down, and that's helping to keep the price from plummeting.

Bitcoin's recent surge has attracted a lot of new attention from investors, who have been looking for an opportunity to make a quick profit.

But the lack of demand for Bitcoins means that if demand for the currency should suddenly start growing, that could send the price crashing back down — as it has done in the past.

If Bitcoin does rise in value, it's likely to become a popular investment for buying things online. Many companies, including Facebook, have said that they're developing their own versions of Bitcoin.

And when Bitcoin does become more widely used, it's likely to have a lot of advantages over traditional currencies.

Bitcoin, for instance, is very difficult to counterfeit, and it's more secure than any other form of money. This is something that people in developing countries are likely to find very attractive.

For people in countries where the currency is under a lot of pressure from inflation, a currency that's easy to use and more secure than regular currency could be a big advantage.

Some countries, like China and Venezuela, have suffered from serious inflation in the last few years, and Bitcoin could be a way for people there to keep their savings safe — or at least to make them less volatile.

Bitcoin could also be a useful tool for making microtransactions with a large number of people. Most retailers can't easily afford to provide discounts to everyone who uses their site. But if someone can afford to buy a little bit of Bitcoin, and then pay some friends for that discount, it could be a relatively cheap way for retailers to try to compete with eBay.

Of course, Bitcoin isn't perfect. It's not impossible to hack, and the fact that there's no central authority making decisions means that Bitcoin is extremely vulnerable to government intervention. The danger of economic chaos in a Bitcoindominated economy isn't too far-fetched.

Another big question is just how popular the currency will become. A lot of people believe Bitcoin has a bright future, but there's no way to know exactly what the future will look like.

It's also very difficult to understand Bitcoin — and the term itself is something of a mystery.

The main reason Bitcoin exists is that some computer experts at academic institutions wanted to experiment with new ways to run digital payments. This led to the creation of Bitcoins, and then the creation of software that allowed them to be exchanged in a secure way.

It's actually relatively easy to understand how Bitcoin works. Here are the basics:

A "miner" in a Bitcoin "mining" process uses powerful computers to solve complex mathematical problems in order to "mine" Bitcoins. The miner gets the number of Bitcoins he's calculated by "mining" if the problem is solved successfully.

Once the miner has a certain number of Bitcoins, he can then send them to people on the Bitcoin network. That's a process called "spending."

You can send Bitcoins to anyone, or create your own Bitcoin wallet.

If you're trying to send Bitcoins to someone, you use a "wallet" to hold Bitcoins, along with a password.

Cryptocurrency wallets.

Want to protect your coins against theft? That's easier to say than it is to do.

Bitcoin has lost more than 50% of its value from last year's highs. Is this the perfect time to jump on board the bubble?

That last question has the media and regulators screaming "yes." According to the New York Times, "the same forces [that are] bringing down the stock market and sending Bitcoin prices down 30% in two weeks could also become the reason for its explosive growth."

Another piece of the media has declared Bitcoin "the money of the future" or the "possible future money of the future." Others simply call it a "bubble." Not so fast.

Bitcoin's fall from grace may be viewed as a case of the old adage, "be careful what you wish for." Just because the media and the regulators say "let's go" with Bitcoin doesn't mean you should just throw caution to the wind.

Smart investors know there's no such thing as "free money." It's more than just the theory of supply and demand at play here. There's a lot more going on here.

First, as most Bitcoiners know, in order to create a new Bitcoin, the miners must solve an equation. This requires a great deal of computational power.

For those who don't know how to program, or don't have the time, a single Bitcoin can take 100 days to mine. This is one of the reasons why in Bitcoin's early days, many Chinese miners were doing so for nearly free.

That free-miner edge has long since dissipated, but it's not only that Chinese miners don't have the raw processing power to mine for Bitcoin anymore. The electricity cost of mining Bitcoin is increasing exponentially. According to recent projections, the cost of electricity for mining Bitcoin is going to increase more than seven-fold by 2019.

In an already volatile market, this is not going to help the Bitcoin story.

And finally, unlike stocks, Bitcoin has no actual value at the moment. It is a speculation, and as most speculators realize, speculation comes with a price.

There are many cryptocurrency holders who see Bitcoin and others like it as "game-changing" and the future of money. These speculators have seen Bitcoin rise more than 13-fold in the past three months. But this time is different. Speculators who are jumping on the Bitcoin bandwagon are late to the game.

85

Conclusion

The basic market of cryptocurrencies.

The biggest and most well known is Bitcoin, the most powerful of the bunch. Although the key to cryptocurrencies are the private, decentralized networks, they can use the same system that bitcoin is based on: blockchain. As the name suggests, blockchain is the distributed ledger that records every transaction and every digital currency transaction.

The use of blockchain has caught on in governments. For years now, blockchain has been proposed as a replacement for the (ever-popular) shadow-banking system, including the Federal Reserve System, which is in charge of most U.S. banking and credit activities. Although no government has yet adopted blockchain, one example of where it is being used is the transfer of medical records through the U.K.'s National Health Service, which is backed by blockchain. Another example is China's health insurance system, which is directly under the Communist Party.

China's central bank is one of the biggest proponents of cryptocurrencies and blockchain. In May, it announced a trial run of its own version of a cryptocurrency known as the China Network Computing System. The government is also looking to launch its own blockchain-based trading platform to revolutionize how it can manage currency transactions.

The move toward cryptocurrencies and blockchain

technologies is being driven by two areas of interest. On one hand, in recent years China and Russia have been looking to update and improve their economies, and it has created a need to understand how blockchain technology could benefit them in the future. On the other, governments are looking to prevent possible cyber attacks, such as those related to the NotPetya attack that was primarily responsible for the fall of major businesses and organizations in Ukraine last year.

Money laundering, tax evasion and the shadow banking system aren't going away anytime soon. Although cryptocurrencies can help with the cost and ease of using cryptocurrencies, the transparency and immutability of the blockchain makes it impossible to recreate that same money. As a result, cryptocurrencies will only gain more legitimacy with time.

Cryptocurrencies can be used as an alternative to traditional money transfers. Another benefit of cryptocurrencies is that they can be transferred between people without the need for a central exchange, such as a bank, which are at risk of being hacked. Cryptocurrency and blockchain-based transactions are also completely anonymous. So, if a government requires transactions on government-controlled currency to be traceable, it can be challenging for a cryptocurrency user to be found.

Cryptocurrencies are extremely safe. The technology that blockchain uses is called decentralized and secure computing. According to a study from researcher David Chaum, there are about 7,000 computers that are regularly checking the blockchain in real time, and those computers are run by hundreds of thousands of people around the world. If one computer fails or if a virus tries to take over the system, it will bring the network to a halt. These kinds of attacks aren't likely to occur, because the blockchain is open source and owned by no one. And this isn't some theoretical assumption. Cryptocurrencies are already used as a safe form of online transfer, and they haven't been hacked in two years.

While it is still in its early days, cryptocurrencies are highly risky investments. While the valuations of cryptocurrencies are rising, the risks of Bitcoin are also increasing. The number of Initial Coin Offerings (ICOs) that are coming out these days is staggering. The value of Bitcoin has dropped significantly since its peak in mid-December of last year.

The long-term future of cryptocurrencies is unclear, but we have at least a few years before it becomes clear. For now, digital currencies are attracting investors, businesses and governments, which is a good thing for all of them. At the same time, governments are doing everything they can to block or regulate the use of cryptocurrencies. This means the future will likely depend on whether or not digital currencies continue to grow in popularity. But with the growing number of dollars flowing into cryptocurrencies, it seems inevitable that they will continue to have a role in the future of the financial system.

In 2014, I predicted the "tipping point" for cryptocurrencies.

I believe we have reached this tipping point. Governments and businesses are not going to sit idly by and allow cryptocurrencies to evolve without their involvement. While most governments are still in the dark about blockchain technology and are unsure how to treat it, I believe they will be coming around soon, because they want to make sure they are still relevant in a world where the average age is almost 10.

This year has been about regulation and the ongoing battle between cryptocurrencies and the governments that wish to control them. But in 2019, the battle will probably shift from governments and Bitcoin to currencies and blockchains built on that technology. This is the same way the internet moved from "somebody else's problem" to a part of every human's daily life in the late 1990s. We are about to enter the "crypto-hubbub" stage.

What are the cryptocurrency market perspectives?

Besides the huge gains this year, there are a few more reasons that make cryptocurrencies attractive:

Governments are not dealing with cryptocurrencies at the moment: Switzerland, Finland, and Estonia are the only nations that regulate cryptocurrencies. However, they do not completely ban them. Even when they do, citizens are left with only limited options.

In the United States, only some states and cities allow crypto transactions. In the U.S., they are still liable for taxes on the bitcoin transaction.

Technology is making cryptocurrency easier to use. There are many sites that allow users to purchase cryptocurrency like bitcoin, litecoin, and ethereum. Cryptocurrencies are available in most countries with easy-to-use web wallets and fiat-to-crypto transactions. The Blockchain, which is behind all cryptocurrencies, is another technological breakthrough that has allowed the use of cryptocurrency for transfer and transfer of ownership.

How to enter the cryptocurrency market?

You can buy, sell, trade or hold the digital currency, buy and sell the token, collect dividend and gain reward.

Cryptocurrency market is not the same as traditional money, where banks maintain the centralized trust. You don't need to trust anyone to sell your cryptocurrency.

As a beginner, you should know that it's not for sure which one is better, at the moment, Ethereum and Bitcoin are the best.

Now, just a few ways of starting your own cryptocurrency.

1. Buy or sell the cryptocurrency itself

Buying or selling the cryptocurrency itself is the most straightforward method, it is quick and easy. The amount of cryptocurrency you'll get in exchange is calculated automatically, if the price is high enough.

The risk is maximum during the beginning; you can lose even your money, if you're not careful.

However, as soon as the service is more stable, there's a lot of possibilities to trade and earn a significant profit.

2. Start an exchange

An exchange is one of the most efficient ways to trade crypto. Most of the exchange services require very little knowledge or effort from their users.

To have an exchange, you must have a partnership with a bank or an institution, that's one of the requirements, but there are other not-so-obvious requirements.

To be a legitimate exchange, you must comply with multiple rules and regulations, from "know your customer" rules, to "know your business" rules.

If you're still thinking about starting an exchange, maybe you're still not convinced, that cryptocurrency exchange is one of the best ways to make money. Don't lose your money.

3. Efficient trading

A solid and fast trading system that generates market prices and the best profit in each and every time of the trading, that's one of the most efficient ways to make money.

You can start a solid mining service, you can start a crypto wallet, you can do everything.

But… what if the market crashes? You'll lose all your money, no matter how advanced your system is.

As the market is volatile, this method is only suitable for experienced traders, and beginners should consider taking some time to gain trust in a reliable exchange.

4. Live trading

This is the only way to get into the crypto market, without

any help from your bank. You have to set up an account with a bank, with minimum KYC and AML policies. It's a tedious and difficult process.

It's best to do live trading, where you can buy and sell digital currency in seconds. This method is available in a number of cryptocurrency trading markets, such as Binance, Huobi and Poloniex.

Cryptocurrency trading tools.

Aspiring cryptocurrency traders could hire a crypto trading expert to help them to place bets on the cryptocurrency market. This is a type of investment broker that will help the investor to trade cryptocurrencies, provide information on which are the best trading strategies for cryptocurrency and offer tips on which cryptocurrency to buy. Trading tips are very crucial for the cryptocurrency trader as it will guide them when and how to go about making these very crucial investments.

Also, there is the option of sending and receiving money through cryptocurrency payment processing platforms. These are the easy to use cryptocurrency payment gateways that will do the work of exchanging fiat currencies for the cryptocurrencies and even give the opportunity of receiving and sending cryptocurrency. They work in a similar way to the PayPal and other online payment solutions, however, they will accept payments in a different currency. The cryptocurrency payment gateways also offer an inbuilt method for depositing cryptocurrency into your bank account.

What are the advantages of trading in cryptocurrency?

These are the various benefits that come with trading in cryptocurrencies, one of them being the transparency in the market. No one can tamper with the market or its currency, therefore, trading in cryptocurrency is very secure and is a very safe option as compared to the conventional way of trading, which is via banks and government regulated currencies. Also, there is no need for the stocks to be invested, because the cryptocurrencies are extremely popular and are able to be acquired with a few clicks.

The main advantage of trading in cryptocurrencies is that they are very low-risk. People are taking up cryptocurrency trading as a career, so it is not surprising that it is gaining popularity among investors. Those who are interested in using this new medium to invest can take up the opportunity. It is very easy to get started with cryptocurrency trading and you don't even need a lot of money to start. Just a few hundred dollars can be enough to get started with and the savings will be very helpful in the long run.